Second Year Report

Director Jamie Rappaport Clark

Conserving the Nature of America

The mission of the U.S. Fish & Wildlife Service is working with others to conserve, protect, and enhance fish, wildlife, plants and their habitats for the continuing benefit of the American people.

Introduction

Director Jamie Rappaport Clark
Tami Heilemann/DOI

A year ago, I issued my First Year Report, challenging the Fish and Wildlife Service to move forward in four priority areas: strengthening our National Wildlife Refuge System; lifting migratory bird conservation to a new level; leading the charge against invasive species; and promoting an ecosystem approach to conservation. In this Second Year Report, I invite all employees to take a look back on 1999, and be proud of how far we've come.

As we begin a new millennium, the four priorities are keeping us focused and on track to meet our goals under the Government Performance and Results Act. For instance, with our new Urban Treaties partnerships and the North American Bird Conservation Initiative, we are making real progress in our effort to sustain migratory bird populations. In 1999, our accomplishments on our National Wildlife Refuges, in our habitat conservation programs, and in our ecosystem team activities all contributed to the greatest effort by any nation in the history of the world to conserve ecologically healthy and diverse habitats for fish and wildlife. And our efforts to improve public use and enjoyment of fish and wildlife paid off with increases in the numbers of Friends groups pitching in at National Wildlife Refuges and greater

voluntary efforts by industry to help keep wildlife safe. Throughout America, ranchers, farmers, and other private landowners are joining hunters and anglers in our efforts to protect the habitat our fish and wildlife need to survive.

Certainly no single report can ever adequately represent all the great things our employees do in a year. The activities highlighted here are just some of the success stories brought about by the hard work and dedication of Service employees. And with the invaluable support of Secretary Bruce Babbitt and Assistant Secretary Don Barry, Service employees have been given the greatest gift of all — the opportunity and encouragement to succeed.

With our momentum and the support of the Interior Department's leadership, we have a chance in this administration's final year to make the turn of the millennium a meaningful moment in the history of the Fish and Wildlife Service. Now is the time to make a concerted push in the four priority areas and also to address some long term needs. Fisheries,

Law Enforcement, Federal Aid — these are crucial programs that need to be strengthened and adapted in order for us to achieve our conservation mission. I intend to dedicate a good deal of my time to help prepare these programs for the challenges ahead.

Sturgeon research.
John and Karen Hollingsworth/USFWS

Partnership with private landowners.
USFWS

Cathy Short

Gary Frazer

Kathy Cheap

John Gottschalk

Lori Williams

Paul Chang

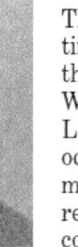

*Senator
John Chafee*

Mamie Parker

Gary Edwards

Illegal wildlife trade products.
Carl Zitsman/USFWS

Archeological training.
Dave Menke/USFWS

To make the most of the opportunities before us, we have some new faces in key leadership roles. In the Washington Office, Cathy Short has taken the helm as the new Assistant Director for our Fisheries Program. Heading the Ecological Services Division, we have Gary Frazer. Former employee Lori Williams has rejoined the Service, this time as Special Assistant to the Director, and Paul Chang from our Law Enforcement Division is the Deputy Director's new Special Assistant. In the Regional Offices, there are some new Deputy Directors: Mamie Parker for Region Five and Gary Edwards for Region Seven.

This is an exciting time to be part of the U.S. Fish and Wildlife Service. Let us use the occasion of the new millennium to renew our commitment to wildlife conservation. In doing so, let us not forget those we lost last year: Kathy Cheap and James "Mike" Callow of Washington's Columbia River National Wildlife Refuge, and Eric Cox of Minnesota's Red Lake Wildlife Management Area — all of whom perished in tragic airplane accidents; Paul Starkey, an enrollee in our Career Awareness Institute who passed away suddenly of a heart seizure; one of our former and greatest directors, John Gottschalk, who lost his life to cancer; and Senator John Chafee, a personal, dear friend of mine and also of the Service, whose leadership on the Hill gave us much to prepare us for the new century. Let us draw inspiration from their memory and commit ourselves to carrying on the mission to which they dedicated their lives.

Setting the Course for the
Future of the Refuge System

Americans have a special fondness for places that are wild and for all that lives there. Our job is to safeguard those wild places and to pass them on to new generations. During the past year, the Service has made great strides in ensuring that our national wildlife refuges are places where Americans can go to learn how wildlife conservation happens, as well as marketplaces of ideas for people who want to help us achieve our conservation goals.

Fulfilling the Promise
The October 1998 Keystone Conference had to be among the most energizing, exhilarating and inspiring events in the history of the National Wildlife Refuge System (NWRS). The 700 delegates to the conference addressed a diverse set of subjects that resulted in a strengthened and reaffirmed vision for the Refuge System. The document which conference delegates produced, "Fulfilling the Promise," provides a detailed road map for the future, giving us the necessary direction for improving the National Wildlife Refuge System well into the next century. Refuge leaders across the country already are making significant progress in implementing the report's recommendations, so the Refuge System can fulfill its promises on behalf of wildlife, habitat and people.

Putting wildlife first
As required by the 1997 National Wildlife Refuge System Improvement Act, the Service issued a draft compatibility policy and regulation that will help us ensure that wildlife comes first when it comes to managing the National Wildlife Refuge System. The draft policy outlines a standard process for reviewing the impacts of proposed and existing public use to ensure that they "do not materially interfere with or detract from" the System's conservation goals. Under this draft policy, refuge managers would be encouraged to offer hunting, fishing, wildlife observation and photography, and environmental education and interpretation opportunities where

compatible with wildlife conservation. In addition to recreation, the policy would also apply to activities conducted as part of a wildlife or habitat management program, such as cooperative farming of grain crops that provide feed for migrating birds.

To meet additional requirements of this landmark conservation law, we published the draft Comprehensive Conservation Planning Policy for public comment. The draft policy directs all refuges to seek public involvement as they prepare plans that will guide decisions on all aspects of refuge operations over 15-year cycles. Under the policy, every refuge or refuge complex must complete a Comprehensive Conservation Plan (CCP) by 2012, and revise each plan every 15 years thereafter, or sooner as necessary. Each CCP will guide management decisions, outline how the refuge will achieve both unit and system wildlife conservation goals, and comply with other requirements such as those for occupational health and safety and access for Americans with disabilities. Each refuge will provide an opportunity for

active public involvement during the preparation and revision of CCPs, including coordination with other Federal agencies, State fish and wildlife and other State agencies, Tribal and local governments, adjacent landowners, and interested members of the public. Sixty-two CCPs, representing 121 stations, are underway, with 27 plans scheduled for completion in FY 1999.

Saving dirt — The role of habitat
As former Director Lynn Greenwalt so eloquently reminded us during the Keystone Conference, the National Wildlife Refuge System is all about "saving dirt." Fortunately, this year we've been able to save some quite important dirt that will help us fulfill our wildlife conservation mission even more effectively in the future. For example, the Service purchased nearly 26,000 acres in northern Vermont from Champion International Corporation as a part of an innovative tri-state land protection partnership created by The Conservation Fund. The Nulhegan Basin was identified as a special focus area in the original plans for the Silvio O. Conte National Fish

Environmental education.
John and Karen Hollingsworth/USFWS

3

and Wildlife Refuge. The biologically-rich area contains significant wetland and extensive areas of uninterrupted forest. It is home to migratory birds, rare, threatened and endangered species protected by the State of Vermont, and resident wildlife, such as deer, bear and moose. Pristine streams flowing through the basin support naturally reproducing native trout populations.

New refuges

The Service added four new refuges to the National Wildlife Refuge System in fiscal year 1999: Aroostook National Wildlife Refuge in Maine; Colorado River Wildlife Management Area (WMA) in Utah; Lost Trail National Wildlife Refuge in Montana; and Navassa Island National Wildlife Refuge, Navassa Island.

Aroostook National Wildlife Refuge is the former Loring Air Force Base, which the Defense Base Closure and Realignment Commission recommended for closure in 1991. Through the Base Closure process and our authority to request no-cost transfers from other Federal agencies, the Service received 4,458 acres of upland forested areas, wetland areas, brooks, beaver ponds, and associated riparian habitat and forested bog systems. This varied habitat supports many species of mammals, amphibians, reptiles, and fish.

The Colorado River Wildlife Management Area has an approved boundary that includes 10,000 acres on the combined river reaches of the Upper Colorado, Gunnison, and Green River systems. It extends into Colorado and Utah. This unit of the National Wildlife Refuge System is the result of a cooperative effort with the U.S. Bureau of Reclamation called the Upper Colorado River Basin Recovery Implementation Program. Our goal and program purpose are to accept conservation easement transfers from BOR for the protection of endangered fishes and fish and wildlife habitat by holding and managing easements as a part of the NWRS. Target fish include the Colorado River pike minnow, razorback sucker, humpback chub, and bonytail. Though most acquisitions for the Colorado River WMA will be through conservation easements, the Service may also protect habitat through cooperative agreements and fee title acquisitions. We established this refuge with the acquisition of 24 easement acres in Utah.

In the nation's heartland, we acquired 9,325 acres in Flathead County, Montana,

Colorado pike minnow.
Hans Stuart/USFWS

to create Lost Trail National Wildlife Refuge. The refuge was established as part of an approved settlement between Interior, Montana Power Company, and the Confederated Salish and Kootenai Tribes as partial mitigation for habitat and wildlife losses associated with Kerr Dam. This area is part of Lost Trail Ranch, which lies in a geographic drainage known as Pleasant Valley, through which Pleasant Valley Creek runs. Wetland habitats abound here, as the Ranch also encompasses the 160-acre Dahl Lake. Upland areas are a mosaic of prairie grasses, wildflowers, and coniferous and deciduous timbered areas. These habitats attract a wide variety of wildlife, ranging from the tiny redside shiner to grizzly bears and gray wolves. Eagles have an active nest next to Dahl Lake.

Navassa Island National Wildlife Refuge is an overlay refuge (meaning we have a secondary interest in the island) through a Memorandum of Understanding with the Office of Insular Affairs, which holds primary jurisdiction. The island lies between Haiti and Jamaica. Two of the island's many plant and animal species that are of particular interest are the white-necked crow and the peregrine falcon. Its waters contain some of the most pristine and healthy coral reefs under United States jurisdiction.

Other acquisitions

On the west coast, the Service worked with the Department of Energy to transfer management of the 60,000-acre Wahluke Slope area of the Hanford Nuclear Reservation in Washington State to the Service, with intent to eventually add the area to the adjacent Saddle Mountain National Wildlife Refuge. We also successfully negotiated for 2000 acres of current and potential endangered shorebird and wetlands habitat for the San Diego Bay National Wildlife Refuge in exchange for 24 acres of endangered shorebird habitat near the San Diego Airport.

Bald eagle.
John and Karen Hollingsworth/USFWS

Gray wolf.
John and Karen Hollingsworth/USFWS

After two years of planning and coordinating among a diverse group of conservation partners in southwest Indiana, the Service also received title to more than 463 acres of wetlands in the Wabash River Bottoms as a unit of the Patoka River National Wildlife Refuge and Management Area. Restoration of this Globally Important Bird Area will include 140 acres of moist soil management units, 50 acres of nesting sites for the federally-endangered interior least tern and over 200 acres of bottomland hardwood plantings. The Service also issued a record of decision in May authorizing the expansion of the Big Muddy National Fish and Wildlife Refuge in Missouri from 16,628 acres to 60,000 acres. The Service will work cooperatively with State and Federal agencies, and other willing sellers to acquire land along the Missouri River floodplain. Restoring this floodplain land should help insure the long-term health of the Missouri River ecosystem.

Refuges in "the Great Land" also made major gains. Through the efforts of the Conservation Fund, the Service received a land donation of 8,500 acres from the Richard and Rhoda Goldman Fund. This donation protects habitat for a wide variety of waterbirds and land mammals on the Izembek and Alaska Peninsula National Wildlife Refuges. We also completed a transaction with the Kenai Native Association that had been in negotiations for nearly 20 years. When the deal was finally done, we'd added 3,245 acres of high value habitat within the Kenai Wilderness Area of the Kenai National Wildlife Refuge.

Connecting people with their wildlife heritage

The U.S. Fish and Wildlife Service opened several new hunting and fishing programs in America's National Wildlife Refuge System over the last year. We proposed 15 new hunting and fishing programs on 11 refuges this August. With these proposed additions, the National Wildlife Refuge System would offer more than 290 public hunting programs and more than 260 public fishing programs.

Many of these refuges celebrate National Fishing Week, National Wildlife Refuge Week, and National Hunting and Fishing Day with fishing derbies and other events that expose the next generation of conservationists to the sport. Our efforts to open refuges to recreational fishing are clearly having an effect. In 1994, there were just over 5 million fishing visits to National Wildlife Refuges each year. By 1998, those numbers surged to almost 6 million fishing visits.

As we opened new refuge hunting and fishing programs, we also took important steps to conserve loons, which spend part of their lives on our refuges. We established 13 refuge "lead-free fishing areas" to protect common loons which are at risk of lead poisoning after swallowing lost or discarded lead tackle. Following a two-year phase-in period, the Service will require anglers to use nontoxic sinkers and jigs in these areas.

This action stemmed from work which began in our New England Field Office in 1994. We've worked together with the North American Loon Fund developing "Let's Get the Lead Out," a brochure encouraging anglers to switch to nontoxic fishing tackle. Recognizing that a number of outreach efforts on the lead issue are ongoing throughout New England, the Service hosted a Lead Sinker Outreach Meeting and brought together

Environmental education.
Dave Menke/USFWS

representatives from seven states, Canada, and the fishing industry

The National Wild Turkey Federation joined us in a new partnership to expand cooperation in the protection, conservation, and management of habitat for wild turkeys and other upland game birds. The Memorandum of Agreement provides a framework for communicating and invites chapters and refuge managers to work together so this partnership can make things happen on the ground.

The Federation became the most recent addition to the host of citizens who are volunteering their time, energy and experience to help the National Wildlife Refuge System. President Clinton signed the National Wildlife Refuge System Volunteer and Partnership Enhancement Act in October 1998, enabling the Service to expand a volunteer network that already accounts for 20 percent of all work performed on refuges and is worth $14 million. The legislation also calls for creation of a Senior Volunteer Corps and provides more flexibility for Refuge staff to work with community partners. This legislation has allowed the Service to take giant steps in three very important areas: the recruitment and use of volunteers, the expansion and use of partnerships, and the simplification of rules governing financial donations to specific refuges.

As always, volunteer and community groups — which provide invaluable local support for individual refuges — continued to display their commitment in

Wild turkey.
Gary M. Stolz/USFWS

a variety of tangible ways. One of the most notable examples of this happened shortly after the Keystone Conference, when the J.N. "Ding" Darling National Wildlife Refuge opened the doors to its new 11,000 square foot visitor center. The visitor center was built by the refuge's cooperating association, the Ding Darling Wildlife Society. Another refuge benefactor, the Sanibel Lions Club, donated a gazebo for placement along the refuge's public bike path, and the Lee Island Coast Tourist Development Council provided funds for the construction of the Shell Mound Trail boardwalk. Similar tangible demonstrations of community support were repeated at refuge after refuge across the nation throughout the year.

Working with our community partners allowed us to host a number of science and cultural camps for rural children,

Volunteer workshop.
Debbie McCrensky/USFWS

National fishing week.
LaVonda Walton/USFWS

mostly Native Alaskans, from the Pribilofs to the Brooks Range. These camps helped refuge neighbors develop knowledge and respect for the ecosystem, cultural resources and the skills required to make informed decisions about local natural and cultural resources.

To inform even more citizens of the wildlife-dependent recreational opportunities available on the Refuge System, the Service prepared a series of six theater slides that began appearing on screens at more than 1,000 movie theaters nationwide, thanks to public service time generously donated by an on-screen advertising company, Century Media Network. In addition to photographs displaying the natural beauty of the System itself, the slides encourage viewers to call the Service's toll-free phone number or visit an online website to learn more about the Refuges. The "Virtual Visitors Center" website was developed for use as a Refuge homepage to encourage online viewers to visit a Refuge. The site also gives viewers an opportunity to experience what they may see and learn at individual refuges, so they too can share our excitement about these irreplaceable wonderlands.

Enviromental tour.
LaVonda Walton/USFWS

Lifting Migratory Bird Conservation to a Higher Level

Waterfowl populations at record highs

Certainly, a strong focus on habitat has helped our nation's waterfowl populations. The 1999 annual survey of breeding duck nesting areas showed an 11 percent increase in population, directly tied to improved habitat conditions throughout much of their breeding range. While favorable weather conditions had much to do with the improvement, wetland restoration efforts deserve a good share of the credit. Even though we've registered record duck populations for four of the last five years, the need for continued habitat conservation has not diminished. The best way to ensure continued hunting opportunities is to conserve populations by doing everything we can to protect, restore and even rebuild waterfowl habitat.

Building on the successes we've experienced working with America's industries, we've taken significant strides in making the world of modern technologies a safer place for our migratory birds.

For example, last April, I announced plans to improve Service and industry cooperation in reducing avian electrocutions nationwide. Addressing the Edison Electric Institute in Williamsburg, Virginia, I called for expanded training and education to promote voluntary compliance with measures designed to prevent bird deaths; the sharing of the Service's knowledge of bird behavior with manufacturers working on the design of "bird-friendly" power poles; and public outreach to help utility customers understand the problem.

The Service recently stepped up its proactive efforts to prevent electrocutions of migratory birds in the Rocky Mountain region, where urban sprawl and industrial growth have introduced powerlines and poles into areas long inhabited by eagles and other raptors. These large birds of prey are

Mallard with brood.
USFWS

particularly vulnerable to electrocution hazards because utility poles offer them a place to rest, hunt, or nest. Their large wingspans increase the possibility that they will make fatal contact with exposed conductors.

Building partnerships with industry

Over the past two years, Service special agents working on this effort have identified areas where birds are dying, alerted the utility industry or the land management agencies that are responsible for the hazardous poles, and worked with these groups to find remedies. Avian electrocutions can usually be prevented by adopting available bird protection measures. This year, U.S. District Judge Lewis T. Babcock issued a landmark legal opinion that concluded that both the Migratory Bird Treaty Act and Eagle Protection Act provide a basis for prosecuting utility companies and other businesses whose activities harm protected birds. His findings came in a case that involved ignored warnings and repeated violations by one western power company. Babcock placed the company on probation for

Rough legged hawk.
John and Karen Hollingsworth/USFWS

three years, ordered it to retrofit utility lines and to pay $100,000 in fines and restitution for the electrocution of eagles and other raptors that landed on its powerlines.

On a related front, we began working with the telecommunications industry to identify the reasons why an estimated four million birds are currently being killed every year in North America in collisions with communications towers. As demand for new towers grows, and technological changes require even taller towers, bird deaths at these sites are an increasing problem that could threaten the health of some migratory bird populations. The Service co-hosted a groundbreaking, first-of-its-kind workshop this August at Cornell University, Ithaca, NY, to examine the growing problem of fatal bird collisions with communications towers. The workshop brought together experts from across the country to discuss the problem and begin forging a course of action in partnership with industry.

Our collaborative efforts with American industry don't end there. The Migratory Bird Management Office and Champion International are conducting a field test of species-habitat models in the spruce-hardwood forest that covers northern New England and the Canadian Maritime Provinces. Large private and public landholders make daily decisions concerning management of large landscapes with little understanding about the consequences to wildlife management. Species-habitat models provide a scientific basis for predicting the outcome of alternative management actions on all wildlife, not just migratory birds. Species-habitat models were developed by a joint Service — USDA Forest Service project for 330 species of birds, amphibians, mammals, and reptiles natural history data. Predictions are based on these models and GIS data for wetlands, soils, topography, and vegetative structure. Comparisons will be made between model predictions and field data collected by refuge biologists on Moosehorn, Nulhegan, Sunkhaze Meadows, Petit Manan, Aroostock, and Lake Umbagog refuges, and private biologists on Champion lands. Validated and refined models will allow biodiversity maps to be estimated for various landscape management scenarios for the present and 25, 50, and 100 years after management.

Seabird conservation

Acting in the international arena, the Service has also helped to ensure a better future for seabirds. The first global plan of action specifically designed to reduce the bycatch of seabirds in commercial fishing gear, which was negotiated in part by representatives of the Service, sets an extremely important precedent for international bird conservation this year. Member countries of the United Nation's Food and Agriculture Organization (FAO) established concrete and specific steps to improve the conservation of 61 species of seabirds known to be killed by taking bait from commercial longline fishing gear. The steps approved by the FAO have the potential to reduce the

Thick-billed murres.
John and Karen Hollingsworth/USFWS

bycatch of seabirds by up to 80 percent or more at national, regional, and global levels.

A collaborative effort by the Chesapeake Bay/Susquehanna River Ecosystem and the Delaware River/Delmarva Coastal Ecosystem Teams in cooperation with the Atlantic States Marine Fisheries Commission's Shad and River Herring Management Board indicated that the bycatch of migratory birds in gillnets may be a significant conservation issue. Through the work of these ecosystem teams, the Service was alerted to the need for a nationwide approach to deal with the bycatch of migratory birds in gillnets and other similar types of gear.

The Service already is taking cooperative actions to address bycatch on longline fishing vessels in Alaska, which are responsible for killing thousands of seabirds each year. Through a cooperative effort with the University of Washington Seagrant Program, we are evaluating the use of paired tori lines — colorful streamers mounted on the back of a fishing vessel — as a cost-effective visual seabird deterrent device. The Endangered Species Act's Landowner Incentive Program provided funding to test paired tori lines in FY 1999. Beginning early in FY 2000, we will be offering free streamer kits to vessel owners who request them, hopefully reaching all of the 2,000-3,000 vessels in the fleet.

Urban bird conservation

Urban birds provide the only day-to-day contact with nature that many city dwellers enjoy. To help cities focus their bird conservation efforts, the Service and the City of New Orleans joined forces to sign the first Urban Treaty for Bird Conservation. The Urban Treaty program will provide a framework to support education programs, habitat restoration and enhancement, and other initiatives mutually agreed upon by the Urban Treaty city and the Service, in consultation with State wildlife agencies. Cities that sign an Urban Treaty for Bird Conservation with the Service may be eligible for matching grants, technical and educational assistance and other support. The Service will also work with the city to find other conservation partners for Urban Treaty initiatives.

Backyard bird feeder.
Nan Rollison/USFWS

Canada geese.
LaVonda Walton/USFWS

Overabundant species

Unfortunately, the type of habitat that attracts birds in urban areas — such as parks, golf courses and lakes — can be too attractive to some species of birds. The Service is faced with management issues posed by rapidly expanding populations of urban and resident Canada geese.

This June, the Service provided States struggling to cope with growing resident populations of Canada geese in urban and suburban communities with greater flexibility to implement population management actions. This new rule streamlined the Service's existing permit process to give State wildlife agencies the opportunity to design their own management programs and to take actions to control specific populations without having to seek a separate permit from the Service for each action. The permits provided under this new rule will allow states to act as soon as it becomes apparent that resident Canada geese are a problem. As long as States satisfy the terms and conditions of their State-specific permits, they can implement management actions without seeking separate permits from the Service every time a problem arises.

In Anchorage, where a growing population of migratory urban geese poses increasing safety threats, the Service led the formation of the Anchorage Waterfowl Working Group, a coalition of agencies and NGOs tasked with developing a strategy for goose population management. The annual growth rate of geese has dropped from 15 percent to 6 percent as a result of collecting eggs and donating them to Alaska Native elders as traditional food, relocating goslings to refuges outside of Anchorage, and lethal control of problem geese at airports. An extensive outreach campaign has accompanied the management activities and is producing results.

Snow and white fronted geese.
Robert Fields/USFWS

Most goose-human conflicts in the United States, however, stem from growing populations of resident Canada goose populations which no longer migrate. The Service has begun the process of developing a nationwide management strategy, holding public meetings and preparing to compile a comprehensive environmental impact statement that explores a variety of management options. We must find ways to control and manage populations of these resident Canada geese that also protect migratory populations.

Snow geese continue to threaten breeding grounds

Exploding populations of migratory "white" geese are threatening to overwhelm the arctic breeding grounds on which dozens of migratory bird species depend.

Changes in agricultural practices and the development of refuges along migration routes have resulted in exploding populations of greater and lesser snow geese, as well as Ross' geese. In February, the Service took action to protect fragile arctic breeding grounds in danger of being destroyed by overgrazing from these populations. Populations have more than sextupled since the 1960s, resulting in far more geese than the fragile arctic tundra, with its short growing season, can support. Many bird species that nest in the same areas as the geese show signs of decline or have otherwise been affected, including semi-palmated sandpipers, red-necked phalaropes, dowitchers, Hudsonian godwits, whimbrels, stilt

sandpipers, yellow rails, American wigeons, northern shovelers, oldsquaws, red-breasted mergansers, parasitic jaegers, and Lapland longspurs, among others. In addition, the southern James Bay population of Canada geese is declining, presumably because of habitat degradation caused by light geese.

After extensive consultation with the Canadian government and a rulemaking process that generated hundreds of public comments, the Service published two rules that allowed 24 Midwestern and southern states to take conservation measures aimed at reducing the population of mid-continent light geese. Although the scientific community, State and Federal agencies and most major conservation groups agreed that "letting nature take its course" was an ill-advised response, the Humane Society of the United States sued the Service. Although a Federal District Court judge ruled in favor of the Service and denied a request for an injunction blocking the rules, the court's ruling led the Service to withdraw the rules and begin a full-scale environmental impact statement evaluating long-term options for managing mid-continent light goose populations. Scoping meetings were held this fall, and we hope to publish a draft EIS this spring, with a final EIS scheduled for completion in late summer of 2000.

Concerned that the time required to complete the EIS would permit further habitat degradation, Congress approved legislation directing the Service to reinstate the rules pending completion of the EIS. The legislation was signed by President Clinton in November, permitting states to again take conservation measures in the winter and spring of 2000.

Cormorant management

Responding to increasing concerns about the impact of double-crested cormorant populations on commercial and recreational fishing, habitat and other migratory birds, we are beginning to develop a comprehensive national cormorant management strategy.

The population resurgence of double-crested cormorants has led to increasing concern about the birds' impact on fish resources. Cormorants and certain other waterbirds can have adverse impacts on fish populations at fish farms, hatcheries, and sites where hatchery-reared fish are released — situations in which fish are concentrated in artificially high densities.

Double-crested cormorant.
Rodney Krey/USFWS

The effect of cormorants on fish populations in open waters is somewhat less clear than at aquaculture facilities. While cormorants can, and often do, take fish species that are valued by commercial and sport anglers, these species usually make up a very small proportion of the birds' diet.

The Service's priority is to maintain healthy cormorant populations across the nation. Our goal is to determine the true impact of cormorants on fish and other resources, and to use the best science available to direct future management.

Caspian terns

Working with the Army Corps of Engineers, Columbia River Intertribal Fish Commission and the National Marine Fisheries Service, the Service also developed a management plan to tackle a very different overpopulation problem. These joint efforts paid off in a successful strategy to relocate a population of Caspian terns and reduce its depredation on salmon in the Columbia River.

Caspian tern.
Donald White/USFWS

North American Waterfowl Plan

For the past 13 years, North American Waterfowl Management Plan joint venture partners throughout the continent have been working diligently to conserve waterfowl and other migratory bird populations and their habitats. To date, Federal, State, and local governments, private organizations, and individuals in the United States alone have contributed more than $1.3 billion toward on-the-ground conservation projects. Their efforts have protected, restored, or enhanced nearly five million acres of habitat. I am pleased to say that two new joint ventures will be joining the Plan's family of 13 habitat and two species joint ventures. The Plan Committee has endorsed the formation of an international Sea Duck Joint Venture and expects to officially recognize the San Francisco Bay Joint Venture in November. All of the joint ventures are taking actions to support the visions of the recently updated Plan, which was signed by Secretary Babbitt and the Canadian and Mexican Ministers earlier this year. The Plan calls for a strengthened biological foundation, a landscape approach to conservation which also considers social and economic factors, and a broadening of partnerships to include other bird conservation initiatives and various other community interests.

This year marked the 10th anniversary of the North American Wetlands Conservation Act and its multimillion-dollar Standard Grants Program, managed by the North American Wetlands Conservation Council. In 1999, the Council approved 72 wetlands conservation projects that protected, restored, or enhanced more than 4.6 million acres of wetland and associated upland habitats in North America. Project partners received more than $68 million in grants this year, which they matched with more than $220 million. I have had the opportunity to visit many of the projects funded by the Act, including one in Mexico at the end of last year. At our Council retreat, held in May at the Service's National Conservation Training Center, we took steps to improve the efficiency of the Act's grants program and to expand its scope to the extent allowable by law. The Act also has a Small Grants Program for conservation projects requiring $50,000 or less. In 1999, the Council approved 21 projects for a total of $732,000 in grants. Project partners matched that with $3.9 million to protect, restore, or enhance 5,400 acres of habitat.

Cooperative efforts with our counterparts in other agencies, and other nations, are providing many successful venues for migratory bird conservation. The North American Waterfowl Management Plan has provided us with an effective framework to work across borders on migratory bird conservation. This year, the North American Office established the Sonoran Desert Joint Venture, the nation's first joint venture with the role of delivering habitat conservation for all North American birds under national/international bird conservation plans. Based on the Western States Partners in Flight Plan, the new joint venture will operate to conserve threatened habitats in the Sonoran Desert region of the United States and Mexico.

Harlequin duck.
Glen Smart/USFWS

Sunset in Sabino Canyon.
Gary M. Stolz/USFWS

In the international arena, we have taken steps to ensure that migratory birds return to the United States year after year. Winged Ambassadors, a bird conservation initiative here in the Western Hemisphere, helps local Caribbean resource managers conserve key bird habitat and provides training in bird conservation techniques. The program also promotes environmental education programs that help communities recognize the tremendous cultural, biological, and economic value of their native bird populations. This year, I was pleased to co-chair an event with the Ambassador of Jamaica, which announced an expanded partnership with the Jamaican government to produce educational materials vividly documenting the value-added benefits their native birds provide. Jamaica has more endemic bird species than any other island in the Caribbean. And from September to May, almost two-fifths of the songbirds in Jamaica are migrants from North America.

Law enforcement

The Division of Law Enforcement improved protections for migratory birds through proactive partnerships, traditional investigative efforts, and regulatory change. Service special agents investigated high-profile crimes involving the large-scale slaughter of protected birds, completing prosecutions and plea agreements that yielded significant fines and restitution. Solved cases included the July 1998 shootings of more than 850 double-crested cormorants on Little Galloo Island in New York. A joint investigation by the Service and the New York Department of Environmental Conservation resulted in the conviction of 10 defendants, who pleaded guilty to their involvement in the killings and were

Hunting.
USFWS

sentenced in United States District Court in Syracuse.

In a move that will promote migratory bird habitat restoration efforts and make it easier for hunters to comply with Federal and State regulations, the U.S. Fish and Wildlife Service announced revised regulations governing migratory game bird baiting for the first time in more than 25 years. The rule gives landowners the flexibility to maintain, develop, manage, and hunt wetland habitat essential for migratory birds without fear of violating Federal regulations that prohibit hunting over areas where seed or other feed has been exposed or scattered. Wetland conservation on private lands is essential to the long-term survival and growth of waterfowl and other migratory bird populations in North America. This

change will provide additional habitat for birds and increase opportunities for hunting over restored and enhanced wetlands, a crucial incentive for landowners that benefits a wide range of species.

Reducing threats from environmental contaminants

The Division of Environmental Contaminants completed a review of chlorfenapyr (Pirate) registration under the Federal Insecticide, Fungicide, and Rodenticide Act, by providing information on impacts to endangered species, migratory birds and aquatic resources. Due to the Service's participation, EPA is carefully reconsidering full registration. Pirate was found to be one of the most reproductively toxic pesticides to birds that the EPA has ever considered for registration. This information provided by the Service to EPA strengthened use restrictions and reduced the potential impact to Service trust species and habitats.

Service biologists, chemists, and law enforcement agents, working with the State of Florida and other Federal agencies, identified organochlorine pesticides as the cause of migratory bird mortality in an area north of Lake Apopka. The quick response to this emergency situation resulted in the reduction of further mortality to endangered wood storks, great blue herons, white pelicans, and other fish-eating birds. Remediation of the site continues in order to provide future habitat for these, and other, migratory birds.

Wood storks.
John and Karen Hollingsworth/USFWS

Leading Efforts to Combat Invasive Species

Many scientists believe the spread of invasive exotic species is one of the most serious threats to biodiversity. Invasive animal and plant species have caused billions of dollars worth of damage to crops and rangeland and have caused other problems, such as the clogging of water pipes by zebra mussels in the Great Lakes region. These are America's "least-wanted" species. They threaten our food, our water and potentially, our health.

Since the passage of the Nonindigenous Aquatic Nuisance Prevention and Control Act of 1990, the Service has been a leader in the war on aquatic invasive species. The Service played a guiding role in the development of the Executive Order, signed in February 1999, which will enhance the coordination of all agencies to address invasive species and link to the existing efforts within the Service. Announced by Interior Secretary Bruce Babbitt, Secretary of Agriculture Dan Glickman, and Under Secretary of Commerce James Baker, this coordinated effort should help curtail the growing environmental and economic threat posed by invasive plants and animals non-native to the ecosystems in the United States.

Shortly after that announcement, the Aquatic Nuisance Species (ANS) Task Force met to discuss strategies for preventing the spread of the zebra mussel into the western United States and a wide range of other invasive species issues. The committee's discussions also addressed the Chinese mitten crab, an aggressive Asian species that was first discovered in California; the round goby, a bottom-feeding European fish that rapidly replaces other native species; and the management of discharges of ballast water used by freighters, a major source for invasive species introduction.

Through recent budget initiatives, the Service is expanding its leadership role to include terrestrial invaders, a focus on

Zebra mussels on native mussel.
Ashville Field Office/USFWS

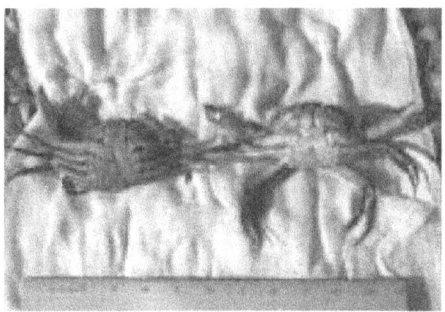

Chinese mitten crabs.
Jon Gilstrom/USFWS

preventing spread through international borders and an increased focus on the numerous aquatic invasives. This cross-programmatic focus has allowed the Service to enhance leadership, take direct action to prevent and control invasives, and raise awareness of invasive species impacts to all Service audiences.

Zebra mussels
The Service developed its "100th Meridian Initiative: A Strategic Approach to Prevent the Westward Spread of Zebra Mussels and Other Aquatic Nuisance Species," which was approved by the ANS Task Force in 1999. This is the first comprehensive and strategically focused effort to prevent the spread of zebra mussels and other invasive species into the west involving Federal, State, Tribal, and Provincial entities. The multi-component initiative will be implemented over a 5-year period and includes such

strategies as voluntary boat inspections and boater surveys, inspections of commercially hauled boats, and evaluation of impacts.

In 1999, the Service began to implement many of the Initiative's components. Posters, brochures, and stickers were produced as part of a larger information and education campaign which targets recreational boaters, those who use personal watercraft, and anglers by informing them about ANS issues and how they can help prevent their spread. Voluntary boat inspections and boater surveys were conducted in the 100th Meridian states, which encompass North and South Dakota, Nebraska, Kansas, Oklahoma, and Texas, and in Manitoba. The program completed its second year, staffed by State resource agencies. Boat education stations were located at strategic locations on western highways and lakes from Manitoba south to Texas. To date, zebra mussels have not been successful in breaching the 100th Meridian.

Building partnerships
The Service is building partnerships throughout the United States to combat the economic and ecological impact of aquatic and terrestrial invasive nuisance species. For the first time, the Service has loaned a senior manager to the Western Governor's Association. Our loaned employee is working to create and implement a comprehensive invasive species management strategy pursuant to the Western Governor's 1998 resolution on terrestrial and aquatic invasive species.

Working through the ANS Task Force, the Service also provided funding for five State ANS Management Plans and is assisting and encouraging the development of at least five more. The Fisheries Regional Invasive Species Coordinators provide technical assistance to the States and Interstate entities in developing and submitting these plans to the ANS Task Force for approval.

The Service, working on behalf of the ANS Task Force, has been leading the effort to develop national survey methods to ensure consistency and comparability among aquatic invasive species surveys throughout the U.S. The Service has also funded surveys in San Francisco Bay, Florida, and the Chesapeake Bay to identify whether aquatic invasive species threaten the ecological characteristics and economic uses of these areas. This information will be critical to assist in the identification of "hot spots" where invasive species threaten aquatic biodiversity.

To enlist the support of a broader segment of the American public in assisting us with these control measures, the Service is developing a public education campaign centered around the theme of "America's Least Wanted" with a poster and press kit featuring TV personality John Walsh from the "America's Most Wanted" TV series.

Efforts in the Great Lakes region
I'm pleased to note that the Service is leading by example in addressing the biological threats posed by invasive species. For example, we're keeping tabs on the round goby, a native of central Asia, in an attempt to keep it from moving out of the Great Lakes and into the Mississippi River navigation system. Along with a host of partners, we're

Round goby.
David Jude/USFWS

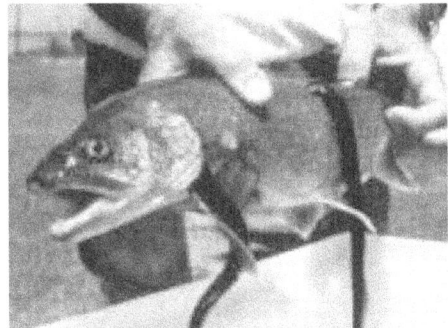

Sea lamprey on apache trout.
USFWS

planning to install an electrical fish barrier in the Chicago Ship and Sanitary Canal next year to help limit the spread of the goby and other nonindigenous fish between the Great Lakes and the Mississippi River Basin. Even then, we'll need to keep our eye on round goby distribution in the Chicago-area waterways to evaluate the effectiveness of the electrical fish barrier and the need for additional control measures.

Also on the Great Lakes, we're looking into the possibility that male sea lampreys from the Atlantic could be used to build the supply of sterile males in the Great Lakes. Using sterile males has helped control the invasive sea lamprey population in the past. Right now, we're using all of the reasonably available male sea lampreys in the Great Lakes area. The study begun this year should help us determine if we can safety and effectively use Atlantic lampreys to continue this successful approach to controlling invasives.

Florida projects
Refuges in Florida, including Egmont Key and Chassahowitzka, are making concerted efforts to remove Brazilian pepper, which forms a thick cover that chokes native vegetation. In addition to attacking the Brazilian pepper, Florida Panther NWR also held an invasive plant species workshop. More than 110 persons representing government agencies and private industry attended to discuss more effective methods to control invasive species.

Brazilian pepper plant.
George Gentry/USFWS

In cooperation with the City of Sanibel, Florida's J.N. "Ding" Darling refuge, established an invasive non-native plant disposal site. This site is used by permitted contractors to dispose of exotic vegetation removed from private property on the island. There is no charge for using this site. City and Refuge employees work together to maintain the site. On the west coast, the Service completed an Integrated Pest Management Plan for Leased Land Agriculture at Lower Klamath and Tule Lake refuges. We worked closely with the U.S. Dept. of Agriculture on this plan, leading to significant achievements in the biological control of saltcedar and integrated weed management, and received the first permit issued for the release of the saltcedar leaf beetle into field cages.

Law enforcement
Service wildlife inspectors and special agents prevented the importation and introduction of invasive species through rigorous enforcement of the injurious wildlife provisions of the Lacey Act. Law enforcement staff helped the South Pacific Regional Environmental Program forge an international partnership to tackle invasive species issues in Oceania, and contributed to protocols to keep Hawaii's new Kahului airport from becoming a conduit for unwanted wildlife and plants. Law Enforcement proposed a framework for new U.S. legislation that would allow emergency listings and increase fines and penalties for importers. A planned expansion of the Service's canine inspection program promises improved interdiction of invasive species at the Nation's ports and border crossings. Outreach to educate other regulatory agencies, such as the Food and Drug Administration, about the dangers of invasive species laid the groundwork for a united Federal effort to close U.S. borders to injurious animals and plants.

Coastal Program
In Puget Sound, the Coastal Program is involved in many invasive species activities. The program is working with Washington State on plans for monitoring and control of the European green crab, including a volunteer effort to monitor the occurrence of the crab in Puget Sound and the strait of Juan de Fuca. The Service is also a member of the education committee of the British Columbia/Washington Exotic Species Work Group and is assisting in the design and funding of outreach materials. In addition, the Service is contributing to an

Oregon coast.
Tom Nebel/USFWS

Bald eagle.
Dave Menke/USFWS

inter-agency effort to implement spartina control measures in northern Puget Sound.

In Southern California, the Coastal Program granted $15,000 to the Baquitos Lagoon Conservancy to remove exotic plants from the lagoon, located in northern San Diego County. A suite of non-native plants, including pampas grass, salt cedars, giant reeds and castor bean plants, had invaded the higher salt marsh intertidal zone, displacing significant areas of valuable habitat. The non-governmental organizations brought their own "in-kind" contribution to match the Coastal Program funds, and in partnership with the State land manager, implemented a more effective project to benefit sensitive resources.

In Delaware, the Coastal program has been involved in many activities to educate the public on the importance of using native plants in habitat restoration projects. On Bombay Hook NWR, the Coastal program has developed a display garden to showcase common native plants on the refuge and present them in landscape setting suitable for residential uses. The program has also worked with several partners in Pennsylvania to develop a "Gardening with the Natives" workshop, as well as a training session at the national meeting of the American Institute of Architects called "Conservation Landscaping with Native Plants."

The Coastal Program in Maine is also doing its part to address invasive species issues. In addition to salt marsh and wetland restoration projects involving

control of common reed and purple loosestrife, they are also working to restore native fish populations. Through river restoration projects, native fish like alewives and the Atlantic salmon are being reestablished and are able to compete better with non-native fish species.

Partners for Fish and Wildlife

In Hawaii, which confronts the most pervasive invasion of non-native species in the nation, half of the biota is not native. The Partners for Fish and Wildlife Program has worked with private landowners to restore many Hawaiian habitats degraded by invasive species. Activities include constructing exclusion fences, implementing animal control measures and growing and planting native plant species. These activities benefit a host of endangered plants and animals which reside in Hawaii's delicate island habitats.

The Partners for Fish and Wildlife Program has also been active in Florida, another place where invasive species are causing severe problems. The Service recently completed five projects in South Florida involving projects to eradicate and control invasive species on 216 acres and 1.1 miles of riparian habitat. Collectively, these projects benefit many threatened and endangered species including the wood stork, snail kite, bald eagle, and eastern indigo snake. These activities also contribute to the South Florida Ecosystem Team's Ecosystem Plan.

Restored Blackfoot Valley wetland.
Rick Dornfeld/USFWS

In Montana, the Partners for Fish and Wildlife Program continued work in its Blackfoot Ecosystem Demonstration Weed Management Area. In the Blackfoot River watershed, the Service continues to bring together a diverse group of land management agencies, county weed control officials, State agencies, and private landowners to develop and implement a cooperative, integrated approach to vegetation management. The program has helped sponsor a number of workshops and tours to promote integrated weed management and has also contributed funds for the release of biological weed agents.

Strengthening the Ecosystem Approach

When I became Director, I promised that I would visit all of the Service's regions as quickly as possible to gain a greater appreciation of the issues you face and to see the Service in action on the ground. Even though I had spent most of my career with the Service, I still came away amazed and impressed by all of the good work I had seen. My next goal was to visit as many of the ecosystem teams as possible. I am still working on that goal, but one thing remains constant. Regardless of whether I visit these teams in the field or hear them brief the directorate on what they have achieved, I continue to be inspired by what these teams have accomplished by building on the strong foundations of ecosystem management on which the Service was built.

The scrub jay population monitoring and habitat restoration at Merritt Island National Wildlife Refuge is one impressive example of what the ecosystem approach can accomplish for our wildlife resources. Staff and funding constraints had prevented the Refuge and the Jacksonville Ecological Services (ES) Field Office from undertaking a comprehensive monitoring program for the threatened scrub jay. In addition, more than a thousand acres of potential scrub jay habitat on the refuge had become overgrown and the refuge lacked the funding, personnel and equipment to aggressively pursue restoration of the habitat. The North Florida Ecosystem Team jointly identified scrub jay habitat as one of their highest priorities. More than 30 Service employees from Refuges, Ecological Services and Fisheries descended on Merritt Island NWR this past spring to carry out the population survey. By combining equipment and personnel from several refuges with Ecological Services funding to address additional equipment needs, the Ecosystem Team restored more than 1,000 acres of habitat.

In another impressive demonstration of cross-program potential, the Roanoke/ Cape Fear/Tar/Neuse Ecosystem Team took on the task of completing a multi-refuge Comprehensive Conservation Plan that goes beyond refuge boundaries to include most of the drainage of the Albemarle and Pamlico sounds, including a portion of southeastern Virginia. The effort includes 11 refuges, two states and two Service regions. Through the Ecosystem Team, the refuges combined efforts to provide the staff needed to lead the effort. In addition, Ecological Service and Fisheries staff will provide significant staff support. Here again ecosystem teams are effectively meeting resource needs.

Klamath River basin

The Klamath/Central Pacific Coast Ecosystem Team has played a significant role in efforts to improve water quality at Agency Lake in Oregon's Klamath River Basin. In recent decades, the Agency Lake has warmed and produced huge algae blooms as the lake and its tributaries were tapped for irrigation, and as agriculture and timber harvest intensified in the watershed. Those problems came to a head in 1988, when the Service listed the shortnose and Lost River suckers as endangered, citing the decline in water quality and quantity in the basin as major reasons for the decline.

Klamath river, CA.
T.A. Blake/USFWS

Upper Klamath NWR.
Ed J. O'Neill/USFWS

An opportunity to improve the situation occurred when Congress appropriated funds for the Bureau of Land Management to purchase the 3,200-acre Wood River Ranch on the lake's north shore. Congress did not provide funds for restoration, necessitating the creation of a broad partnership of Federal, State and Tribal agencies, conservation groups, and private landowners. The project has demonstrated that the Service doesn't have to be the lead agency on a project to achieve ecosystem team goals.

Several facilities from the Service's Klamath/Central Pacific Coast Ecosystem Team contributed to this effort, anteing up people power, expertise, and dollars from the Hatfield Program, and the Partners for Fish and Wildlife and Jobs-in-the-woods programs. The BLM managed a public timber sale for the Service's Klamath Basin Refuge Complex, allowing the Service to plow the proceeds back into the restoration effort. The partners reflooded thousands of acres of heavily-grazed former pasture, and are in the process of reconstructing the banks of the lower Wood River to restore wetlands and provide more water to the lake. Temperatures in the lake have already dropped several degrees, and the numbers of waterfowl using the lake have expanded twentyfold.

Great Lakes

The Great Lakes Basin Ecosystem Team has also made a difference, creating the lake sturgeon research Internet homepage (http://www.fws.gov/r3pao/sturgeon), which provides background information, calendars, contact numbers and extensive sturgeon-related links. The homepage serves as a nexus for groups working to conserve this prehistoric fish. The Great Lakes team also served as a resource for Congressional inquiries during the reauthorization of the Great Lakes Fish and Wildlife Restoration Act.

Waterfowl hunting.
Mike Hemming/USFWS

Fishing.
Tami Heilemann/DOI

Leadership in Natural Resources Conservation

I'd like to turn now to other programs and initiatives that made significant progress in 1999. The Fish and Wildlife Service is made up of thousands of dedicated professionals, each of whom plays and important role in our success as an agency and as a steward of our natural heritage. My only regret is that there are too many achievements to review in this short document. We've tried to touch on the most prominent success stories, but I know there is much we left out.

Saving Endangered Species

Late in 1998 we celebrated the 25th anniversary of the Endangered Species Act, one of the driving forces which leads us toward the ecosystem approach to fish and wildlife conservation. The law's purpose is to conserve "the ecosystems upon which endangered and threatened species depend" and to conserve and recover listed species. It is a challenge which encompasses not only familiar and beloved mammals, birds, and fishes, but also little-known plants, amphibians, reptiles, insects, and crustaceans. But the worthiness of the law's broad purpose has become more apparent over the years, as scientists have found the value of rare plants and animals as sources for new medicines and genetic reservoirs for new agricultural crops. We've also begun to see more and more evidence that our decades of hard work are improving the lot of our nation's wildlife.

One of the most remarkable events of 1999 was the announcement that the peregrine falcon had graduated from the list of endangered and threatened species. The Peregrine Fund, the Raptor Center, the Santa Cruz Predatory Bird Research Group, states and many volunteers worked with the Fish and Wildlife Service over the last two decades to successfully breed and release peregrines into the wild. Once near extinction, their numbers have reached 1,593 breeding pairs, inhabiting skyscrapers, bridges, and cliffs in 40 states.

Many more species followed the peregrine on the road to recovery over the past year, including our national symbol, the bald eagle, the Aleutian Canada goose, and the Tinian monarch.

The proposal to delist the Tinian monarch, a tiny flycatcher found only on the island of Tinian in Commonwealth of the Northern Marianas Islands, came as non-native forests grew back on the island. If the proposal is finalized, this will be the fourth Pacific bird species removed from the protection of the Endangered Species Act due to its recovery.

The proposed delisting of the Aleutian Canada Goose is an Endangered Species success story unlike any other. The bird's recovery is a result not of a single action or recovery effort, but of a suite of recovery efforts by a network of dedicated individuals. The eradication of introduced foxes from nesting islands in the Aleutians, implementation of hunting restrictions and development of sanctuaries on the geese' wintering grounds in California, Oregon and Washington paved the way for recovery.

Tinian monarch.
© Jaan K. Lepson

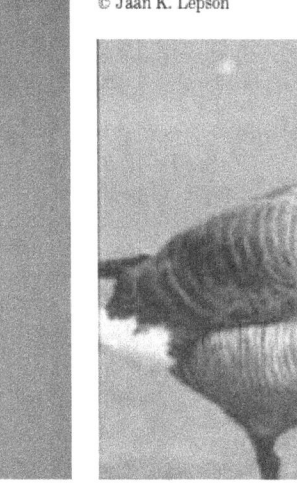

Aleutian Canada goose.
Glen Smart/USFWS

Peregrine falcon.
Ted Swem/USFWS

Bald eagle ceremony, proposal for delisting.
Tami Heilemann/DOI

Preserving our nation's symbol

On the eve of Independence Day weekend, President Clinton marked the culmination of a three-decade effort to protect and recover the majestic bald eagle by announcing a proposal to remove it from the list of threatened and endangered species. The bald eagle once ranged throughout every State in the Union except Hawaii. When America adopted the bird as its national symbol in 1782, as many as 100,000 nesting bald eagles lived in the continental United States, excluding Alaska. By 1963, only 417 nesting pairs were found in the lower 48. Today, due to recovery efforts by the Service in partnership with other Federal agencies, Tribes, State and local governments, conservation organizations, universities, corporations and thousands of individual Americans, this number has risen to an estimated 5,748 nesting pairs.

Wolf Recovery

Continued successes in our recovery program offer hope that many other species will eventually graduate from the list of endangered and threatened species. The combined efforts of the Service, the states and Tribal conservation agencies have helped wolf population numbers in the Upper Midwest reach the recovery goals set back in 1978. The Service is now engaged in a careful evaluation of the wolf management plans submitted by State and Tribal governments to ensure they support the long-term viability of wolves. A decision by the Service to remove wolves from the Endangered Species List or change their status will be made only after a complete review of all public comments and wolf management plans,

Gray wolf.
LuRay Parker/USFWS

including those related to the management of wolves in the western United States.

Despite repeated setbacks and the shooting deaths of five of the Mexican wolves originally reintroduced into southern Arizona, this remarkable recovery effort continues. Some of the reintroduced packs are reproducing in the wild, offering us hope that this species too can return to playing its vital role in the southwest's ecosystem.

South Florida multi-species recovery

This May, Secretary Babbitt and the Service's Southeast Regional Director Sam Hamilton presided over a landmark signing ceremony implementing a Multi-species Recovery Plan in Boca Raton Florida. This event marked a major step toward South Florida Ecosystem restoration and the recovery of threatened and endangered species in South Florida. The Multi-species Recovery Plan is one of the first and most far reaching ecosystem plans developed by the Service. It serves as a blueprint to recover 68 threatened and endangered species, and to restore and maintain biodiversity of native plants and animals in the 23 natural communities throughout about 26,000 square miles of the 19 southernmost counties in Florida.

Black-footed ferret

The State, Federal, Tribal and private members of the Black-footed Ferret Recovery Implementation Team continued to make major strides in this species' recovery. Captive and on-the-ground efforts have resulted in the production of nearly 500 ferrets, the highest number on record. There are now more ferrets in the wild than in captivity. A partnership effort with the City of Ft. Collins, Colorado, is under development

for the construction of a new captive breeding facility and a new partnership with the Turner Endangered Species Fund resulted in a new captive breeding facility on the Turner Ranch in New Mexico.

Making the Endangered Species Act work better

To promote consistency, flexibility and streamline processes in our dealings with other Federal agencies, we issued the final Endangered Species Consultation Handbook: Procedures for Conducting Consultation and Conference Activities Under Section 7 of the Endangered Species Act. The handbook provides information and guidelines on the various consultation processes outlined in government regulations and is intended to promote consistent implementation within and between the Service and the National Marine Fisheries Service (NMFS).

Also in conjunction with NMFS, we proposed guidelines to strengthen the use of habitat conservation plans (HCPs) as a conservation tool. The guidelines incorporated the knowledge gained over the last four years to improve the way HCPs are developed and administered in five areas: establishment of measurable biological goals and objectives, use of adaptive management, monitoring, public participation, and determination of the duration of the incidental take permits. We have more than 240 HCPs in effect and more than 200 under development. In FY 1999, the Service completed 20 HCPs covering 14.2 million acres.

HCPs are a particularly popular conservation tool in our nation's rapidly growing and changing west coast, where eight HCPs had been approved during the first nine months of this past year.

Black footed ferret.
M.R. Matchett

Attwater's prairie chicken project.
Nancy Moriaty/USFWS

Two forest HCPs and associated permits were provided: one to the Pacific Lumber Company, including the largest tract of old-growth redwood forest remaining in private ownership, and another to the City of the Dalles, Oregon, which covered more than 200,000 acres. The six non-forest HCPs that were completed covered 4,891 acres, and ranged in size from 6 to 3,465 acres.

Safe Harbor

Because the majority of endangered and threatened species occur on privately owned land we published joint final policies with NMFS for "Safe Harbor" and "Candidate Conservation Agreements with Assurances" to provide incentives for non-Federal property owners to work with us in species conservation. The "Safe Harbor" policy provides incentives for private and other non-Federal property owners to restore, enhance, or maintain habitats for listed species. Under the policy, the agencies provide participating landowners with technical assistance and assurances that additional land, water, and/or natural resource use restrictions will not be imposed as a result of voluntary conservation actions that benefit or attract listed species. At the end of a "Safe Harbor" agreement, the landowner would be allowed to return the property to its original "baseline" condition.

The "Safe Harbor" policy is already making a difference on the ground, and has become an important tool in the recovery of the Attwater's prairie chicken, one of North America's most endangered birds. The Attwater Prairie

Red-cockaded Woodpecker Safe Harbor Program.
Lori Duncan/USFWS

Chicken National Wildlife Refuge and Texas Nature Conservancy's Galveston Bay Coastal Prairie Preserve can only support a limited number of prairie chickens. Therefore, the success of the Attwater's recovery program depends upon the cooperative efforts of private landowners. The Sam Houston Resource Conservation and Development Area, Inc. and local Soil and Water Conservation Districts instituted a program directed at the restoration and enhancement of coastal prairie habitat on private lands. To ease landowner concerns about habitat enhancement leading to Endangered Species Act liabilities, a habitat conservation plan was prepared — including a "safe harbor" provision — for the Attwater's prairie chicken. To date, cooperative projects involving 8 willing landowners have been implemented to restore 17,800 acres of coastal prairie habitat. An additional 4 landowner agreements

totaling more than 22,000 acres are pending. Interest in this program has mushroomed to the point landowners are put on a waiting list until additional funds become available.

Landowner Incentive Program

Beginning in FY 1999, Congress authorized $5 million for the Endangered Species Landowner Incentive Program to provide long-sought financial assistance and incentives to private landowners for voluntary conservation agreements that benefit listed and candidate species through Safe Harbor Agreements and Candidate Conservation Agreements with Assurances. An overwhelming total of 145 proposals for $21.1 million were submitted for funding in FY 1999. Twenty-two projects were selected for full or partial funding. The selected projects involve a variety of conservation actions and regulatory assurance agreements for a number of listed species.

Among the projects is the South Carolina Red-cockaded Woodpecker Safe Harbor Program, in which 21,802 acres will be managed with fire, 260 acres of longleaf pine will be planted, and 172 artificial nesting cavities installed. Twenty-three properties are included in this program. In another example, Boise Cascade Corp. is in the process of drafting an agreement to manage property in northern Idaho to conserve the northern Idaho ground squirrel. Other landowners throughout the area are interested in developing similar agreements.

Candidate Conservation Agreements with Assurances

The Service and NMFS also released their final policy on "Candidate Conservation Agreements with Assurances" (CCAA) for species that are not yet listed as endangered or threatened, but are considered to be in decline and could be listed in the future. Through CCAAs, landowners commit to take actions that conserve declining species. These actions may include habitat protection; management; or restoration actions such as fencing, stream rehabilitation, controlled burns, or species reintroduction. Landowners who participate in this program will receive assurances from the agencies that no additional conservation measures above and beyond those contained in the CCAA will be required and that no additional land, water, or resource-use restrictions will be imposed upon them should the species become listed in the future.

Mountain plover.
Fritz L. Knopf/USFWS

The American shad, once the most common fish in the James River in Virginia and found in abundance in neighboring Maryland, dwindled over the years as dams splintered its spawning grounds. Thanks to a huge coalition of private, Federal, State and civic organizations, the shad's habitat is being restored and the Harrison Lake National Fish Hatchery is lending a critical hand in this species' recovery, which looks better today than it has in years.

The Gila trout, already an endangered species, may well become a recreational fish, thanks to the work of the Mescalero and Mora National Fish Hatcheries and the New Mexico Fishery Resources Office. The Gila trout was reintroduced in both Arizona and New Mexico this year and biologists are optimistic for the species' future.

Here too, the policy is already providing measurable improvements in wildlife habitat. The lesser prairie chicken has been the focus of the High Plains Partnership. With ESA Landowner Incentive Program Funding, the Service is working with landowners to develop CCAAs. Voluntary conservation plans adopted this year on private land will restore 16,000 acres in New Mexico and 35,000 acres in Oklahoma. The declining swift fox, mountain plover, long-billed curlew, and burrowing owl, among others, are expected to benefit from these measures, as well as the black-tailed prairie dog. More than thirty landowners are currently on the waiting list to participate.

Law enforcement

Although cooperative habitat preservation efforts with industry and landowners yielded many success stories, the Service continued to seek sanctions against developers who ignored endangered species protections. In California, for example, special agents worked on investigations involving the unlawful take of coastal California gnatcatchers, Morro shoulderband snails, California red-legged frogs, Tipton kangaroo rats, and two federally protected plants — all cases involving construction or other activities that destroyed or modified species habitat.

Designating Critical Habitat

Finally, we began taking steps to explore methods of fully complying with the ESA's critical habitat requirements in a way that will allow us to spend our limited resources in a manner that will provide the greatest conservation benefit to as many species as possible. Protection of habitat is paramount to successful conservation and recovery of threatened and endangered species. But the designation of critical habitat under the Act has provided little additional protection to most listed species while consuming significant amounts of funding, staff time, and other resources. By taking the initial steps to invite public involvement in this process, we hope to improve the process by which critical habitat is designated.

Restoring Aquatic Species and Habitat

The National Fish Hatchery system has continued a vigorous effort to restore native fish species that have wide recreational value.

Paddlefish restoration

The paddlefish, a species in decline that we were concerned might need the protection of the ESA, is making a comeback. This fish, found throughout the Mississippi River drainage from the Upper Missouri River to the Louisiana Delta, is in far better shape today thanks to the restoration work of the Garrison Dam, Tishomingo and Private John Allen National Fish Hatcheries. Their populations are expanding, through stocking, beyond dams that once impeded spawning runs.

The Willow Beach NFH successfully completed research studies and propagated and cultured more than 200,000 razorback suckers, 50,000 bonytail chub, 100 humpback chub and 25,000 Colorado pikeminnow. Work at San Marcos National Fish Hatchery located the exotic snail and associated

Gila trout.
Kim Mello/USFWS

Paddlefish.
Galen Buterbaugh/USFWS

parasite that has been damaging the endangered fountain darter in the Comal River of West Texas. The San Marco hatchery also maintained a Texas wildrice refugium, began more native aquatic plant culture and restoration programs, and provided a refugium for the recently listed Comal Springs riffle beetle. The Texas blind salamander, which has been held there since 1991, released eggs for the first time on station in January 1999. Further east, artificial spawning efforts produced the first successful spawning of the robust redhorse in Georgia's Savannah river. The fertilized eggs were transported to the Warm Springs NFH and to the McDuffie State Fish Hatchery in Georgia, and also provided to State hatcheries in South Carolina.

Threats to aquatic species
As many of the accomplishments cited earlier indicate, some of the most remarkable achievements in habitat restoration have been in aquatic habitats. Freshwater habitats in the U.S. contain some of the most threatened groups of species. For example, more than one-third of freshwater fishes and amphibians dependent on aquatic or wetland habitats are at risk; two-thirds of freshwater mussels and crayfishes are rare and imperiled; one in 10 mussels may become extinct during this century; and 110 freshwater fish species are listed as threatened or endangered. Although the threats to aquatic species vary, we do see consistent threads — intensive water resource development, pollution, and habitat loss. The Fisheries program is conducting 38 aquatic habitat restoration projects across the country involving 29 states. These on-the-ground projects involve more than 100 partners and are restoring 460 miles of riparian habitat and 3,850 acres of in-stream and wetland habitat.

Breaching Edwards Dam
One of the most dramatic improvements in aquatic habitat came on July 1, 1999, when Maine's Edwards Dam, built in 1837, was breached without public expense, opening 17 miles of the Kennebec River to nine migratory fish species. Secretary Babbitt, two governors and the entire congressional delegation of Maine took a personal interest in securing the removal. Service employees, through the Northeast Hydro Program, played a decisive role in the historic and precedent setting decision. The Northeast Region was a strong advocate of removal, participated in negotiations with the owners, and provided substantial evidence that restoration goals could not be met by installing fishways. The Service's efforts helped increase fish resources available for people in the future.

For the first time in 160 years, nine species of migratory fish will again have free access to their historic habitat, including Atlantic salmon, American shad, American eel, endangered shortnose sturgeon, Atlantic sturgeon, alewife, blueback herring, striped bass, and rainbow smelt. The river corridor above the dam is undeveloped and offers a secluded atmosphere. Since this free-flowing, non-tidal, riverine ecosystem is being restored within proximity of the State capital, economic benefits to the local and regional area are expected.

The decision was heralded on the front page of leading newspapers across the county and on National Public Radio. This decision embodies the realization that a dam is not necessarily a permanent feature of the landscape, that dams have sometimes degraded watersheds, ecosystems, and fisheries, and that dam removal is warranted in certain instances.

Identifying fish barriers
The Service is actively developing an inventory of National Fish Barriers that will be useful in identifying dams for either fish passage or removal. In the Northeast Region alone, the Service estimates that there are over a million barriers in waters that either block or severely impact movement of aquatic species — barriers that often result in significant population declines, and even listing under the ESA. These barriers not only affect migrant fish, but many resident fish, freshwater mussels, crayfish, insect, amphibian and reptile species as well. When completed the

Edwards dam.
USFWS

Fish ladder.
USFWS

inventory of barriers will describe the type of impacts and species and amount of habitats affected.

Sometimes all we need to do is modify existing passages. Changes to the Cocheco River Fishway on the Merrimack River in New Hampshire, provided passage for anadromous fish and a donor source of river herring for extensive high priority restoration efforts in the Merrimack River. This project will significantly increase use of the fishway and assist in the cooperative effort between the Service and the New Hampshire Fish and Game Department to enhance runs of anadromous fish species in the Cocheco and Merrimack Rivers and other New Hampshire coastal rivers.

In other cases, we must work with others to modify the flows provided through existing dams. The Service, as lead agency, completed the Trinity River Flow Study report, an 18 year cooperative effort with Bureau of Reclamation, Trinity County and the Hoopa Tribe that outlines a scientifically based program of modified flow regimes and mechanical restoration to bring back one of California's premier anadromous fish

Fishing at Loxahatchee NWR.
John and Karen Hollingsworth/USFWS

streams, and important trust assets of the Hoopa Tribe. As one of the Department's lead agencies, the Service continues to play a key role in the CALFED negotiations, a critical ecosystem approach to water use and environmental restoration and enhancement.

Sport Fishing and Boating Partnership Council

In 1998, work by the Service's Sport Fishing and Boating Partnership Council helped launch a congressionally mandated national public outreach campaign designed to encourage more Americans to boat, fish and develop a commitment to conserving our nation's aquatic resources. The 5-year, $36 million campaign is being administered by the Recreational Boating and Fishing Foundation under a cooperative agreement with the Service.

The Sportfishing and Boating Safety Act of 1998 directed the Secretary of Interior to develop, in cooperation with the federally chartered council, a national outreach plan to encourage greater public interest and participation in boating and fishing. The plan also aims to provide more information about recreational boating and angling opportunities, reduce barriers to participation in these activities, and promote conservation and the responsible use of aquatic resources. During the spring and summer of 1998, the council sponsored an extensive series of regional and national public meetings to identify issues that hamper boating and fishing.

Following the stakeholder meetings, the council named an outreach planning team to distill the raw data and draft a plan. The resulting Strategic Plan for the National Outreach and Communication Program was completed Sept. 15, 1998, and approved by Interior Secretary Babbitt Feb. 23, 1999. A cooperative agreement establishing the framework for Federal funding of the foundation was signed March 28, 1999, during a ceremony at the North American Wildlife and Natural Resources Conference in Burlingame, Calif.

Other habitat restoration activities

The Service has also focused on a variety of habitat restoration activities in both the Ecological Services and Fisheries

programs. For example, Partners for Fish and Wildlife is working on native trout restoration in the northern Rockies. Partners in on-the-ground projects in Montana's Blackfoot Valley, Centennial Valley, Graves Creek, and Yellowstone River, and in Wyoming's Wind River basin are leveraging Service dollars at a four to one ratio. All partners recognize that targeting native trout for restoration is in reality using an indicator species approach to ecosystem management. Instream, riparian, and upland restoration measures for trout are instrumental in also restoring habitat and survivability of mammals, migratory birds, imperiled amphibians, and plant communities.

Similar efforts are underway on both coasts to promote salmon recovery. Through these partnerships, 71 miles of stream were opened up to anadromous fish in the Pacific Region. The Portland-Vancouver Metro Area Greenspaces Program successes involved restoration of 5 acres of wetlands, 22 miles of riparian and instream habitat and 27 acres of upland habitat associated with other trust species. Fifty miles of stream were opened to anadromous fish and 54 acres of off-channel rearing habitat were restored for salmon. The Service is also working with other Federal regional executives to develop solutions to Columbia River salmon problems, including a 1999 decision on operating the Federal dam system in compliance with the Endangered Species and Clean Water Act, and as a member of the Interagency Salmon Science Team charged with science-based salmonid restoration.

Pink salmon.
G. Hahnel/USFWS

King salmon.
Mary Smith/USFWS

Partnership programs in Alaska also focused on riparian habitat important for spawning and rearing salmon. Alaskan restoration partnerships were recognized with two of only four national Coastal America Partnership Awards in 1999: the multi-agency/public effort to restore Duck Creek, an impaired body of water flowing through the City of Juneau; and the Kenai River 50:50 Program, a multi-agency/public effort to restore riparian habitat on public and private lands along the Kenai River.

Encouraging sustainable development
Aside from the Partners program, we're making significant progress in protecting habitat for wildlife and encouraging sustainable development. After nearly five years of negotiations involving the Service and Federal and State agencies in Wisconsin, we signed a formal interagency agreement with our partners that will help protect wildlife habitat from secondary land-use changes spurred by a major upgrade of U.S. Highway 12 in the Baraboo Hills region of south central Wisconsin. Among the Service's concerns is the protection of one of the largest contiguous blocks of southern upland forest in the Midwest. The area provides habitat for numerous migratory birds and plant "Species of Concern," including the cerulean warbler, prairie thistle, bog bluegrass and Blandings turtle. The agreement created a local advisory committee made up of all of the partners. The committee will review each phase of the highway project to determine impacts on wildlife resources and to decide on appropriate mitigation.

The Fish and Wildlife Management Assistance Program has had many 1999 successes with habitat restoration in aquatic environments. Examples include notching dikes on the Mississippi River and stabilizing streambeds and wetlands on the Ohio River in order to improve both water quality and substrate habitat for mussels. And in Florida, the program is working with the Division of Refuges to restore tidal flows and functions to 35 acres of coastal marsh at Merritt Island NWR to benefit snook, red drum and many wading birds and waterfowl.

In every case, these success stories were born of cooperation from organizations and individuals outside the Service. We are taking continual steps to make sure that this cooperation not only continues, but increases.

Working with Tribes to Protect Wildlife and Habitat

This fiscal year marked the first time in the history of the service that all regions had a dedicated Indian Desk, working directly with Tribes to implement initiatives and cooperative management of wildlife and habitat across the country. The results of this commitment by the Service are evident in success stories in every region of the country.

On a national level, four years of work on a negotiated rulemaking resulted in completion of the final Tribal Self-Governance regulations. The Native American Liaison acted as the non-BIA lead in the negotiation and finalization of the rule, editing the final version and

addressing all policy concerns identified in public comments. The final rule has been sent to the Tribal negotiation team for their review, with publication expected sometime in early winter of 2000.

The Native American Liaison also served as the Service lead for the compilation of a joint handbook on contracting with Indian Tribes for the Department of the Interior and Health and Human Services' Indian Health Service. The handbook covers all matters for contracting Indian programs to Tribes under the Indian Self-Determination and Education Assistance Act, including the disposition of surplus property and the due diligence required of personnel assigned to oversee such contracts.

Salmon conservation
In the Pacific Region, the Native American liaison held numerous meetings throughout the year with the Puget Sound Tribes, city and county representatives, and the National Marine Fisheries Service to review the conservation strategy for salmonids. The Service also participated in a joint project with the Stillaguamish Tribe, the Adopt-A-Stream Foundation, a private landowner and local conservation districts to restore four acres of wetlands and 20 acres of juvenile salmon-rearing habitat in Washington.

Native fish restoration
In the Southwest Region, the Native American Liaison worked with the Jicarilla Apache Tribe, the Service, the Running Elk Corporation and the New

Flathead reservation fisheries work.
Ron Skates/USFWS

Salmon in "button up" stage.
USFWS

Rio Grand cutthroat trout.
Lloyde Hazzard/USFWS

Mexico Department of Game and Fish to draft a Memorandum of Agreement for management and restoration of the Rio Grande cutthroat trout.

In partnership with 10 other organizations, including a grant from the North American Wetlands Conservation Act, the Liaison worked with the Fond Du Lac band of Chippewa to restore over 1,200 acres of wetland and associated open water habitat in the Great Lakes Region suitable for the production of wild rice. The Liaison also did Tribal surveys and held informational meetings with Tribal members throughout the region in conjunction with the delisting of the gray wolf, lynx, Karner blue butterfly and the massasauga rattlesnake.

The Service's Creston National Fish Hatchery intensified work with the Blackfeet Indian Reservation to restore native Westslope cutthroat trout in streams previously stocked with non-native rainbow trout. The Service and the Tribe continued to collaborate to identify streams best suited for restoration and to modify production programs and schedules at Creston NFH to furnish native Westslope cutthroat trout.

Hatcheries at Alchessay and Williams Creek initiated cooperative discussions with Tribes to pursue opportunities in

Tribal waters of Arizona, New Mexico and Colorado to restore native trout species to waters historically stocked with non-native rainbow trout, brook trout and cutthroat trout, while simultaneously satisfying Tribal trust responsibilities.

Tribal law enforcement assistance
In the Northeast Region, the Service signed a Memorandum of Agreement in April formalizing and broadening the sharing of law enforcement expertise with the Passamaquody Tribe of Maine. The Service and the Tribe will utilize certain officers to enforce Federal and Tribal laws on lands belonging to the Tribe. In September, the Law Enforcement Division conducted training for officers who will perform enforcement duties outlined in the MOA. This is the first such agreement in the region, and should serve as a prototype for similar agreements with other Tribes.

Also in Maine, the Craig Brook and Green Lake National Fish Hatcheries and the Maine Anadromous Fisheries Coordinator coordinate extensively with the Penobscot Indian Nation and the Passamaquoddy Tribes on anadromous fish restoration. Approximately 570,000 Atlantic salmon smolts, 300,000 Atlantic salmon parr, and 1.5 million Atlantic salmon fry were stocked in the Penobscot River, along with 21,000 smolts stocked in the St. Croix River.

Mountain-Prairie Region
In the Mountain-Prairie Region, the Native American Liaison worked with the Ute Mountain Ute Council on the proposed listing of the sleeping Ute milk

vetch. The Service and the Tribe will survey reservation lands for the plant in the spring of 2000, with the Service providing $3,000 to the Tribe for its assistance in conducting the survey.

In the Alaska region, the Native Issues Advisor helped develop a Memorandum of Understanding among Federal agencies in Alaska to coordinate communication efforts with Alaska Natives.

Law Enforcement

Sturgeon are in danger of extinction because of over-harvesting to support a rampant international illegal market in caviar. Two years ago, the Service spearheaded a proposal to give all species of wild sturgeon protection under the Convention on International Trade In Endangered Species (CITES), a treaty that protects globally traded animals and plants from over-exploitation. This year, the Service's Law Enforcement Division worked successfully to uphold these protections and crack down on illegal imports of caviar. Wildlife inspectors and special agents at the nation's major ports of entry seized shipments entering the country without the required export permits and foiled numerous smuggling attempts.

One New York-based case, for example, resulted in the nation's first Federal felony prosecution of a caviar importer for illegal trade. In October 1998, Service Special Agents apprehended seven individuals attempting to smuggle a total of 16 suitcases containing 901 (500 gram) tins of Beluga caviar.

Atlantic salmon.
William W. Hartley/USFWS

Inspecting caviar.
USFWS

Freshwater mussel.
John and Karen Hollingsworth/USFWS

The total weight of the caviar seized was approximately 1,000 lbs, with an estimated value ranging from $675,000 to more than $1.1 million. Three individuals were arrested and charged with violating the ESA and CITES, and with felony conspiracy and smuggling charges. Service Special Agents later executed a Federal search warrant at the Connecticut home of one of the smugglers and seized records and an additional 1,000 lbs. of caviar. Indictments charge that between April and November of 1998, two of the individuals sold approximately 19,000 lbs. of imported caviar to American caviar retailers. During the same period of time the defendants received permission from the Service to import only one shipment of 88 lbs. of caviar.

In November, a jury convicted one smuggler of conspiracy, smuggling, and violating the Lacey Act — a Federal statute that makes it a crime to import wildlife or wildlife products taken, possessed, transported, or sold in violation of any U.S. law or treaty. A second defendant was convicted of one felony violation of the Lacey Act, while a third individual pleaded guilty to conspiracy to smuggle wildlife.

Poaching operations
Service special agents and State conservation officers closed out a major multistate investigation of illegal trafficking in freshwater mussels — a threat to both clam species and ecosystems in the Nation's heartland. The investigation, which broke up a poaching operation spearheaded by the country's second largest shell exporter, resulted in the conviction of the company, its president and vice-president, and six other individuals. Penalties assessed

included more than $400,000 in fines and restitution (including a $250,000 payment from the company) as well as significant terms of imprisonment and probation.

Trophy big game hunters come to Alaska from around the world, making commercial big game guiding — much of it occurring on refuge lands — the State's seventh largest industry. While most guides act professionally and obey wildlife laws, Law Enforcement in Region 7 has continued to monitor hunting on refuges to ensure adequate wildlife protection. Lacey Act investigations in the past year have resulted in eight convictions for violations of the Act, with charges pending against seven other individuals. Fines and penalties of nearly $100,000 have been assessed. One guide was sentenced to a year in Federal prison,

and seven airplanes and numerous wildlife trophies have been seized.

Protecting manatees
Regional law enforcement special agents coordinated six law enforcement task force operations in Florida during FY 1999. The operations were to enforce manatee speed zone laws designed to protect endangered manatees from injury or death by boat strikes. Death by boat strike is the cause of 25 percent of total manatee mortality. Some 46 Special Agents and 12 Refuge Officers took part in these operations that resulted in the issuance of 732 Federal notices of violation (tickets). Each notice carries a $100 fine.

The Service and the Environmental Protection Agency jointly investigated the illegal dumping of nearly 150 tons of mercury chemicals into Georgia coastal marshes. The case resulted in the convictions of 6 individuals and a corporation for violations of environmental laws and the Endangered Species Act. The Federal court imposed sentences totaling: 21 years, 7 months of active jail time, 10 months of home detention, $50,745 in fines, 13 years of probation and 1,390 hours of community service.

Saving the world's coral reefs
The Division of Law Enforcement contributed to U.S. and global efforts to protect coral reefs, nearly 60 percent of which are imperiled by human activity. Enforcement staff chaired the trade subgroup of the Presidentially created U.S. Coral Reef Task Force, directing an

Manatees.
Jim P. Reid/USGS

Fish survey.
Jerry Ludwig/USFWS

interagency effort to analyze U.S. trade data for corals, sea horses, and live reef fish and propose improved trade controls. Service wildlife inspectors took the lead in planning, coordinating, and conducting a marine invertebrate identification workshop for North American wildlife law enforcement officers; this well-received training promises improved enforcement of existing trade laws that protect corals and other marine species at U.S., Canadian, and Mexican ports of entry. Service law enforcement also secured the first Federal felony conviction for coral smuggling in a Florida case that involved illegal trafficking in corals plundered from reefs in the Philippines.

New frontiers in forensic science
Wildlife forensics gained global recognition as a new field of science at the triennial meeting of the International Association of Forensic Sciences, thanks largely to the pioneering research of the National Fish and Wildlife Forensics Laboratory. An unprecedented Service-chaired wildlife forensics section meeting, which included research, casework, and poster presentations from all 14 laboratory scientists, attracted some 100 of the U.S. and international experts in attendance. The laboratory's latest research accomplishments include the discovery that hemoglobin provides a quick and accurate way to identify species, a vital step in analyzing evidence from wildlife crimes. The fast-track development of a DNA method to detect the sturgeon species represented in a tin of caviar proved crucial to Service efforts to protect these endangered fish. Demand for case assistance from Federal, State, and foreign investigative agencies remained high, reflecting the Laboratory's position as the world's first

and only full-service crime lab devoted to wildlife law enforcement as well as its accreditation by the American Society of Crime Lab Directors — a professional status attained by only half of the crime labs in the United States.

Training the world's "Thin Green Line"
In addition to investigating cases, Law Enforcement worked proactively with Ecological Services, Montana State University, Wyoming Outfitter and Guide Association, and the Professional Guide Institute to conduct a bear safety course for guides and outfitters. The course, titled "Safety for People, Safety for Bears: Avoiding and Mitigating Bear Encounters in Grizzly Country" has been well received. Special Agents continued their outreach efforts with landowners and hunters in drainage areas where wolves are present, in an effort to generate support for the release program. As a result of these efforts, wolf mortalities have been significantly reduced in the region.

Region 6 Law Enforcement continues to take the lead on providing law enforcement and forensics training to Native Americans from all across the country. This year training was conducted at the Navajo Law Enforcement Training Center in Toyei-Ganado, Arizona. Thirty-five Conservation Officers completed the 40-hour certified course. The success of this course was attributed to the cooperative efforts of the Navajo Nation, Native American Fish and Wildlife Society and the Service. The second training course was conducted at the Mashanfucket

Pequot Nation during the National Conference of the Native American Fish and Wildlife Society. This training focused on Forensics/Evidence Gathering Techniques, and was again well attended by a variety of Tribal resource managers/conservation officers. To date, the Service has trained over 300 Native Americans across the country.

Service special agents and wildlife inspectors proved the instructors of choice for countries seeking to upgrade their wildlife law enforcement capability. The Division conducted hands-on anti-poaching training for national park rangers in Tanzania in cooperation with the U.S. Agency for International Development and teamed with the Global Survival Network, Wildlife Conservation Society, and Thai Royal Forestry Department to launch an anti-poaching and community outreach campaign in that Asian nation's most famous national park. Service enforcement and international affairs staff joined the U.S. Department of Justice to promote wildlife conservation and improved trade monitoring in Madagascar — an island nation where wildlife resources are increasingly being plundered for the global black market. Wildlife inspectors and Office of Management Authority staff conducted CITES enforcement training for customs officers and wildlife protection officials in China. International enforcement partnerships also included investigative assistance in Kenya, where Service special agents helped probe an organized wildlife crime syndicate preying on elephants, rhinos, and other endangered African animals.

Training in Thailand.
USFWS

International Affairs

Currently more than 100 nations, including the United States, embrace the Convention on Wetlands of International Importance, better known as the Ramsar Convention. Because many wetland habitats span international boundaries and many wetland species are migratory, Ramsar countries preserve wetlands within their own borders while working together to ensure the health of wetlands around the world. The United States recently demonstrated the importance it places on this convention by nominating its 16th and 17th sites — Sand Lake National Wildlife Refuge, South Dakota, and the Bolinas Lagoon, California. Sand Lake is the only Wetlands Convention site within the Prairie Pothole Joint Venture Area, a subdivision of the North American Waterfowl Management Plan. Bolinas Lagoon, managed by the Marin County Open Space District, is a 1,100 acre tidal embayment located as the south end of the Point Reyes peninsula in California — the first wetland to be nominated on the Pacific Flyway in the lower 48 states.

The Service also headed the U.S. delegation to the 7th Ramsar Conference of Parties in San Jose, Costa Rica. Working with the other 116 nations that are parties to the Convention, the U.S. delegation led efforts to improve conservation of wetlands, waterfowl and other wetland species around the world.

CITES
Also, as an international partner in the Convention on International Trade in Endangered Species (CITES), we hosted and chaired an international working group, which drafted the first CITES 5-year strategic plan. Representatives from Zimbabwe, Australia, Colombia, and elsewhere joined us this spring for an intensive four days of negotiations that resulted in the draft document. The strategic plan will be one of many topics discussed at the CITES conference in Kenya in April 2000. The final version will outline the vision and actions that will carry CITES into the next millennium.

Reptiles and amphibians received a helping hand when we hosted the CITES Animals Committee Transport Working Group in Washington. This meeting provided an opportunity for stakeholders to work together to improve humane transport for reptiles and amphibians in international trade. Thanks to this groundbreaking work, the International

Red-eyed treefrog.
Gary M. Stolz/USFWS

Air Transport Association announced new transport standards for reptiles and amphibians. These went into effect globally on October 1.

Changes in scientific permits
To make it easier for our partners in the conservation community to participate in the process of collecting essential data on federally regulated species, we have initiated a top-to-bottom reform of our scientific permits process. Our goal is to make the process for obtaining scientific permits for endangered species, migratory birds, marine mammals, and CITES-listed species serve as an incentive, rather than a disincentive, for contributions to their conservation. There has been an enthusiastic response from the scientific and conservation communities to the reforms, including positive reviews from many respected scientific institutions and the Society for Conservation Biology.

This year, discussions with State and Federal partners, as well as thorough analysis of available biological and trade information convinced us that immediate action was need to help conserve wild American ginseng, the most valuable wild export from the U.S. To prevent overharvesting, we decided to issue export permits only for wild ginseng older than five years of age. Many states and the Forest Service have adopted similar restrictions on harvest, reflecting a true partnership with the Service to protect this valuable and vulnerable species.

Rhinoceros and Tiger Conservation Act
Imperiled wild rhinoceros and tigers now have a brighter future thanks to innovative legislation enacted by the U.S. Congress and signed into law by President Clinton on October 30, 1998. The Rhinoceros and Tiger Conservation Act of 1998 includes an important new product labeling provision that states "A person shall not sell, import, or export, or

Black rhinoceros.
Maslowski Productions/USFWS

Siberian tiger.
John and Karen Hollingsworth/USFWS

attempt to sell, import, or export, any product, item, or substance intended for human consumption containing, or labeled or advertised as containing, any substance derived from any species of rhinoceros or tiger."

Strengthening Our Workforce

Training
In FY 1999, the National Conservation Training Center conducted over 250 training courses for more than 5000 participants. NCTC has continued to expand its curriculum with 140 different courses, 42 of which were new courses developed this year. Participants range from every State in the Nation, more than 100 organizations and 20 international countries. 12,497 people attended events hosted by NCTC, including 1,500 for the open house in October 1998. Of those, 3,881 stayed onsite. Several high profile events were held during the year, including the DOI EEO Conference, the Jefferson County West Virginia Science Olympiad, and the DOI Health and Safety Seminar. Former President Jimmy Carter also visited the site. NCTC also hosted the Fire and Grit Millennium Conference, hosted by the Orion Society and attended by more than 500 participants. The Aldo Leopold Conference, discussing Leopold's conservation legacy, was held during May.

Distance learning
NCTC has increased its emphasis on distance learning, with the development and distribution of correspondence courses, web-based training, CD-ROM courses, video training tapes, satellite conferencing and interactive television broadcasts. The Service has demonstrated its commitment to distance learning by establishing twelve distance learning classrooms across the nation which enables employees to participate in interactive television training broadcasts close to their workstations. Thirty distance learning events were conducted this year reaching approximately 10,000 students.

Diversifying our work force
We have continued our efforts in strengthening and diversifying the work force. This year we took a more holistic approach by looking at barriers that have impeded our progress and to address each specific issue on a Servicewide basis. Our efforts began with the dissemination of our Diversity vision that articulated the objective of a

Distance learning broadcast.
USFWS

Service work force that is reflective of the diversity of the citizenry it serves and the commitment by the entire Directorate through the signed Charter. We have shown results in recruitment, retention and accountability.

Redoubling our pro-active recruitment programs targeting women and minorities
Women and minorities have accounted for 63 percent of our outside hires in the past year. As a result of this emphasis, the total number of minorities within our workforce has increased by 12 percent from last year, with a net gain in our overall representation. Our increased use of the student employment program has been an asset to this effort.

Providing more attention to our career development and retention efforts
Women and minorities receive more than 50 percent of all promotions within the Service, demonstrating our commitment

to diversity. But retaining quality female and minority employees is equally important as promoting them. A Career Development and Retention Work group has reviewed separation data and results of exit interviews and developed recommendations that include specific action steps to address retention and work environment/work place issues.

Holding every manager in the Service accountable
Through specific action items, managers are involved throughout the recruitment, selection and career development process, and progress is monitored regularly.

In the Service's ongoing effort to increase its work force diversity and outreach, several Memoranda of Understanding (MOUs)were signed with various minority organizations, including the National Hispanic Environmental

Partnership signing ceremony for U.S. Fish & Wildlife Service and Historically Black Colleges and Universities.
LaVonda Walton/USFWS

Council, the Hispanic Association of Colleges and Universities, and five Historically Black Colleges and Universities.

The rewards of these agreements are far-reaching for all parties involved. They will provide the Service with the opportunity to increase minority participation in the Service's activities and enhance recruitment efforts. We still have much work to do, but I am pleased that we have shown significant progress this year.

Employee pocket guide

The ecosystem teams are starting to create opportunities for cross-collaboration, and to make this easier for everyone, our National Outreach Team has prepared a Fish and Wildlife Service pocket guide for every employee. Within its pages, Service employees will be able to find information on all programs of the Service and how they can help meet specific needs. This will be an invaluable tool for us all as we create innovative approaches to species and habitat conservation.

Regulation enforcement.
USFWS

Hunter safety course.
George Andejko/AZ Game and Fish Dept.

In Conclusion

In closing, I'd like to thank every Service employee for the dedication you demonstrated over the past year, dedication that is visible in the measurable successes we've achieved. I look forward to working with you over the next year to realize more of our vision for wildlife.

We are on the cusp of a new millennium. This is a symbolic time to renew our commitment to wildlife conservation. But it is also an ideal time for us to take advantage of our good fortune in having support from on high in the administration. The clock is ticking. We have come so far. Now let us finish strong, with powerful, determined strides into a new era.

Fishing.
Carl Zitzman/USFWS

Bird watching.
John and Karen Hollingsworth/USFWS